# Music Publishing

Other Record Labels

otherrecordlabels.com

First Edition, 2023
ORLB14.2

Published by Other Record Labels.

ISBN 9798374622102
Canada


www.otherrecordlabels.com

## Get the Bonus Content

This book tells the story of music publishing and how it relates to independent record labels. It is my hope that it provides more than enough to get you on your way. However, I want to make sure that all the tools and resources I mention in this book are relevant and up to date.

Visit **otherrecordlabels.com/publishing-bonus** for extra resources!

Be sure to join our private community of record labels at **http://facebook.otherrecordlabels.com**

And feel free to email me if you ever have any questions! **scott@otherrecordlabels.com**

# Table of Contents

# Introduction

One of the primary objectives behind what I do with *Other Record Labels* is to "take the mystery out of running a record label." This goal exists because there are some parts of the music industry that are confusing, intimidating, and often hidden behind gatekeepers. If you've ever been afraid of asking a "stupid question" you're in luck... I've already asked them for you!

This book is tailored specifically for independent record labels and independent artists looking to navigate the complex and ever-changing landscape of the music industry. In this book, you will learn about the various aspects of music publishing, from songwriting and copyright to licensing and distribution. Whether you're just starting out or are a seasoned veteran, this book will provide you with the knowledge and tools you need to successfully publish and promote your music in today's market.

More importantly, I hope to help take the mystery out of music publishing, to make it less intimidating, and to provide you with a basic understanding. The music industry has many facets, there is a lot to learn, and while not a comprehensive textbook, this book is meant to help provide the basics of music publishing. We'll cover terminology, frequently asked questions, the basics of copyright, and publishing royalties.

If I've done my job right, you will have gained a solid overview of how music publishing works as it relates to indie record labels. My hope is that we can use the pages that lay ahead to help demystify the world of music publishing.

# CHAPTER ONE

# MUSIC PUBLISHING COMPANIES EXPLAINED

A music publishing company is a business that owns and manages the rights to a collection of musical compositions and licenses the use of those compositions to other parties, such as record labels, film studios, and other music users. They are responsible for protecting the rights of the composers and songwriters and ensuring that they receive royalties for the use of their work. They also promote the compositions to potential licensees and may work to place the compositions in various forms of media, such as films, commercials, and television shows. They may also be responsible for administering and collecting royalties for the compositions and for ensuring that the compositions are properly registered with performance rights organizations.

## Owning and Managing Musical Composition Rights

Music publishing companies acquire the rights to the compositions from songwriters and composers and become the legal owner of those rights. They then license the use of those compositions to other parties such as record labels, film studios, and other music users.

## Promoting the Compositions

Music publishing companies actively promote the compositions in their catalog to potential licensees, through direct pitches, networking, and even attending industry events to showcase the songs and composers they represent.

## Administering and Collecting Royalties

Music publishing companies are responsible for ensuring that composers and songwriters receive royalties for the use of their work. They do this by administering the collection of royalties, tracking the usage of the compositions, and making sure that the compositions are properly registered with performance rights organizations. They then pay the royalties to the composers and songwriters.

**Action Step**

For a massively comprehensive guide to all things music industry related (including the basics of music publishing), check out the book, "All You Need to Know About the Music Industry" by Donald S. Passman. http://otherrecordlabels.com/books

CHAPTER TWO

# UNDERSTANDING MUSIC METADATA

M usic publishing metadata refers to information about a song or composition that is used to identify, track, and manage the rights and royalties associated with the work. This information is typically stored in a database and is used by music publishers, performance rights organizations, and other industry organizations to ensure that the proper parties are compensated when the work is used.

## Basic Metadata

Basic Metadata can include simple things like lyrics, genre/style, release date and song title. Including all songwriters and co-writers is also essential in collecting the metadata surrounding a specific composition.

## Understanding ISRCs

An ISRC (International Standard Recording Code) is a unique identifier that is assigned to a specific recording of a song. It is used to identify and track the use of that recording in various contexts, such as in music streaming services or in royalty calculations. The ISRC is typically embedded in the audio file of the recording and is also recorded in the metadata of the recording when it is distributed. The format of an ISRC is standardized and is managed by the International Federation of the Phonographic Industry (IFPI).

**Understanding ISRWs**

An ISWC (International Standard Musical Work Code) is a unique identifier assigned to a specific musical work by a performance rights organization or other industry body. It is used to identify and track the rights and royalties associated with a particular song or composition, and to ensure that the proper parties are compensated when the work is used.

*The ISWC code is made up of four parts:*

- the first three characters (T-prefix) indicate that the code is an ISWC

- the next six characters are the country code

- the next nine characters are the publisher code

- the last six characters are a unique identifier for the specific work.

**Action Step**

Start a spreadsheet in Google Sheets or Excel where you keep your record label's entire song catalog strictly organized. Include columns for ISWCs, ISRCs, songwriters, genres, subgenres, production credits, and more. This will help you not only with music publishing tasks but future sync licensing opportunities.

# CHAPTER THREE

# THE BASICS OF MUSIC COPYRIGHT

M usic copyright is the legal protection given to the creators of original musical works. It gives them the exclusive right to reproduce, distribute, and perform their work for a certain period.

## The Basics of Music Copyright

Music copyright is the legal protection that is given to the creators of original musical works. This protection gives the creators of musical works the exclusive right to reproduce, distribute, and perform their works publicly. This means that others cannot use the work without permission from the copyright holder.

## How Music is Automatically Protected

When a musical work is created (and subsequently recorded on paper or as a sound recording), it is automatically protected by copyright. The copyright holder has the exclusive right to make copies of the work, distribute the work, and perform the work publicly. They also have the exclusive right to create derivative works, such as making a new arrangement of a song, or to license others to use the work. Copyright protection for a musical work lasts for the life of the creator plus a certain number of years after their death.

## The Difference Between Sound Recording and Songwriting

It's important to note that while a sound recording is also protected by copyright, it is distinct from the copyright of the songwriting. The copyright holder of a sound recording has the exclusive right to reproduce and distribute the recording, while the copyright holder of the songwriting has the exclusive right to reproduce, distribute and perform the songwriting publicly. Additionally, the copyright holder of the songwriting also has the right to authorize others to make sound recordings of the song. As a result, there could be different rights holders for the songwriting and a sound recording of the same song.

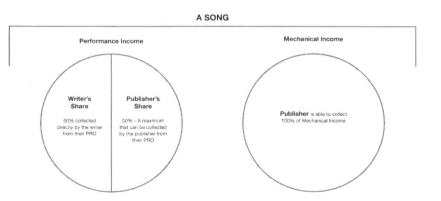

A SONG

Performance Income

Writer's Share
50% collected directly by the writer from their PRO

Publisher's Share
50% - A maximum that can be collected by the publisher from their PRO

Mechanical Income

**Publisher** is able to collect 100% of Mechanical Income

**Action Step**

Americans can easily register their copyrights by visiting www.copyright.gov/registration

CHAPTER FOUR

# THE BASICS OF PUBLISHING ROYALTIES

Music publishing royalties are payments made to songwriters and publishers for the use of their musical works. They can be earned through the sale of recordings, performances, and the use of the music in other media such as film and television.

**Understanding Mechanical Rights**

Music mechanical royalties refer to the royalties that are paid to the songwriting copyright owner or their publisher when their songwriting is reproduced in the form of a physical or digital copy, such as a CD, vinyl, mp3, or streaming service. These royalties are paid to the copyright owner when their songwriting is manufactured, distributed, and sold by third parties. The copyright owner can either collect these royalties themselves or through a publisher or Performing Rights Organization (PRO).

The rate for mechanical royalties is typically set by law and can vary by country. In the United States, the rate is set by the Copyright Royalty Board. The mechanical royalty rate for physical formats, such as CDs, is currently 9.1 cents per song for songs that are 5 minutes or less and 1.75 cents per minute for songs over 5 minutes. For digital formats, such as streaming and downloads, the rate is a percentage of revenue that varies depending on the service. The copyright owner can negotiate a different rate through a direct license agreement, but such agreements need to be approved by the Copyright Royalty Board.

## Understanding Performance Royalties

Music performance royalties refer to the royalties that are paid to the song's copyright owner or their publisher when their songwriting is performed publicly, such as on radio, television, live performances, or streaming services. These royalties are also paid to the copyright owner when their song is performed by third parties. The copyright owner can either collect these royalties themselves or through a Performing Rights Organization (PRO) like ASCAP, BMI, and SESAC in the United States, or similar organizations in other countries.

The rate for performance royalties is typically set by law and can vary by country. In the United States, the rate is set by the Copyright Royalty Board. The performance royalty rate for traditional broadcast like radio and television is currently set at 1.75 cents per song per play. For streaming services like Spotify, Pandora, and YouTube, the rate is a percentage of revenue that varies depending on the service and the agreement with the copyright holder.

## Understanding Sync Fees

A sync fee, short for "synchronization fee," is a payment made to the copyright holder of a songwriting or sound recording when the work is used in a film, television show, commercial, or other audio-visual production. This fee is paid for the right to use the copyrighted music in synchronization with the visuals in a production. This can include using the songwriting or sound recording as background music, in the soundtrack, or as part of the score.

Sync fees can vary greatly depending on the type of production, how the music is used, and the specific terms of the agreement. Factors such as the budget of the production, the prominence of the music in the production, and the size of the audience that the production will reach can all affect the sync fee. A sync fee for a major film or television show can be quite substantial, while a sync fee for a regional commercial or independent film may be relatively small. Sync fees are negotiated between the copyright holder and the production company.

Sync licensing fees refer to the payment made

to a copyright holder for the use of a specific piece of music in a film, television show, commercial, video game, or other visual media. These specific fees are typically paid by the production company or advertising agency that is using the music. However, the copyright holder of the music – usually the music publisher or the artist themselves– will also need to be paid. Sometimes an artist will negotiate an "all in" fee which includes both the sync fee and the publishing fee. Other times, a publisher will also need to negotiate their fee with the production company or agency.

**Understanding Recording Royalties**

Recording royalties are payments made generally from record labels to artists for the use and distribution of recorded music. These royalties are generated when music is sold (such as on physical albums or digital downloads) or streamed on platforms like Spotify, AppleMusic, or Pandora. The amount of royalties earned will depend on the terms of the artist's recording contract with the label, and typically, the label will take a percentage of the revenue as a distribution or marketing fee. The artist will then receive the remaining royalties as payment for their performances on the recordings. It's important to note that recording royalties and publishing royalties are different, and the latter refers to the payment made for the use of the underlying composition, not the recording of it.

**Action Step**

To go deeper on this topic, check out the book "The Plain and Simple Guide to Music Publishing" by Randall D. Wixen http://otherrecordlabels.com/books

# CHAPTER FIVE

# STARTING A PUBLISHING COMPANY

Starting a music publishing company can be a good way for a record label to ensure that they are able to maximize the revenue potential from the songs they release. Having said that, it is not a simple process, and should not be taken lightly.

## The Pros of Starting a Publishing Company

Record labels should always be looking out for additional revenue streams to support their long-term sustainability. A publishing company can act as a new and viable revenue stream if executed properly.

*Some things that may entice you to set up a publishing arm of your record label...*

- The ability to collect and distribute royalties from the use of the songs in various media such as film and television.

- The ability to control and exploit the rights to the songs for other uses such as merchandise and live performances.

- The ability to license the songs for use in other media and to other recording artists.

## The Cons of Starting a Publishing Company

Too many start-up record labels underestimate the arduous task of setting up a proper publishing company. If a record label intends on taking a cut from their artists' songs, they need to ensure they are earning their percentage!

*Some things that may give you pause when considering launching a music publishing arm of your record label...*

- The additional cost of setting up and running the publishing company.

- The need to manage and administer the publishing rights and royalties.

- The risk of being liable for any copyright infringement that may occur.

## Getting Help with Your New Publishing Company

Starting a music publishing company can be a complicated process as it requires knowledge of legal, financial, and business aspects of the music industry. It may also require a significant investment of time and money. It is best for a record label to consult with a lawyer, accountant, and a music business expert before deciding on starting a publishing company.

**Action Step**

Before starting a publishing company, take a listen to this interview I did with a music publishing expert from 3tone Music Publishing.

otherrecordlabels.com/publishing

# CHAPTER SIX

# TYPES OF PUBLISHING AGREEMENTS

**N**ot all publishing agreements are made equal. The artists on your record label may have the opportunity to sign a variety of different publishing deals. In this chapter, I want to briefly outline the three most common publishing agreements a songwriter may encounter.

## Exclusive Songwriter Agreement (ESA)

An Exclusive Songwriter Agreement (ESA) is a contract between a songwriter and a music publishing company, where the songwriter grants the publishing company the exclusive right to administer, exploit and protect their compositions in exchange for royalties and other forms of compensation. It typically covers all compositions, for a certain period, and the publishing company is responsible for registration, collection of royalties, promotion, and administration. It's important for songwriters to understand the terms and have legal representation before signing.

## Single Song Agreement

A Single Song Agreement is a contract between a songwriter and a music publisher, where the songwriter grants the publisher the right to exploit, administer and protect specific songs or a limited set of songs in exchange for royalties and other forms of compensation. It's different from an Exclusive Songwriter Agreement (ESA) as it covers only specific songs or a limited set of songs rather than all the songwriter's compositions.

**Publishing Administration Agreement**

A Publishing Administration Agreement is a contract where a songwriter or copyright owner grants a publishing administrator the non-exclusive right to administer, register, collect royalties and promote copyrighted material on their behalf in exchange for a percentage of the royalties as compensation. The administrator also provides administrative support, legal representation, and other services. It's important for songwriters or copyright owners to understand the terms and have legal representation before signing.

---

**Action Step**

If you need to hire a music attorney, check out our Directory of trusted music industry vendors and service providers. These are folks who are friends with *Other Record Labels* and who many of our community members have worked with in the past! Go to otherrecordlabels.com/directory

# CHAPTER SEVEN

# KEEPING YOUR MUSIC CATALOG ORGANIZED

Keeping your record label's music catalog neatly organized can allow you to be prepared for future publishing opportunities that may come your way.

## The Importance of Tracking Royalties

Keeping a catalog organized allows the record label to track royalties and ensure that artists are being paid correctly for all uses of their music. This is important for maximizing publishing profits as it ensures that the label is receiving all the royalties it is entitled to.

I always recommend record labels check out a platform called, Infinite Catalog, a royalty management company designed specifically for indie labels: otherrecordlabels.com/royalties.

## Being Prepared for Licensing Opportunities

Having a well-organized catalog makes it easier for the record label to identify potential licensing opportunities for their music. This can include film and television placements, syncs, and other commercial uses of the music.

You can be more prepared for various licensing opportunities when your catalog is organized by genre, theme, emotion, tempo, or key.

Organizing the catalog makes it easier for the label to manage and leverage their assets. It allows them to have a clear overview of what is available for licensing and sync opportunities, and to track and report on the use of their music. It also makes it easier for the label to identify and exploit new opportunities and revenue streams.

## Managing Your Promotional Assets

In addition to organizing your song catalog, it is also important to keep track of your promotional assets, ideally in a centralized location (Dropbox, Google Drive, etc.).

Promotional assets can include press photos, lyrics, album artwork, MP3 and WAV files, instrumental versions, web banners, artist bios, and more.

## Action Step

*I have a free organizational tool that's included in my Sync Licensing Toolkit. This spreadsheet template will help you stay organized, not only for music publishing purposes, but for other revenue opportunities like Sync Licensing. Check it out here: otherrecordlabels.com/sync*

# CHAPTER EIGHT

# CONNECTING YOUR ARTISTS WITH A LOCAL PRO

A record label can assist their artists in registering with their local Performing Rights Organization (PRO) by providing them with information on the registration process, helping them to gather the necessary documentation, and possibly even covering the cost of registration fees.

## Educating Your Artists About Publishing

A record label can provide their artists with information about the registration process for their local performing rights society, including any requirements or documentation needed for registration.

Some PROs offer regular workshops for artists and indie labels that may benefit you and the artist to attend.

Similarly, select PROs have in-depth info sessions on YouTube that may help walk you and your artists through the complicated world of publishing and performance royalties specific to your country.

## Assisting Your Artists with Registering

Record labels can also help their artists gather the necessary documentation for registration, such as proof of copyright ownership or a list of compositions.

Once you become familiar with this registration process, you'll be able to assist the future artists more easily on your label.

**Financially Assisting Your Artists with Getting Registered**

Finally, some record labels may also cover the cost of registration fees for their artists, which can be a significant financial burden for independent musicians. This can also serve as an incentive for artists to register with their local performing rights society and/or to sign to your record label.

---

**Action Step**

It might also be a good idea to help educate your artists on the world of music publishing. Summarize what you've learned in this book or at conferences and provide the artists on your label with a summary of the basics of music publishing. It is not necessary for artists to understand the whole scope of this topic, but it is important that they know their rights and the role they play.

---

# CHAPTER NINE

# PRO BASICS

Performing Rights Organizations are key to the publishing success of your artists. Labels should be aware of their local PRO, why they exist, and how to assist their artists with registering with their local PRO.

## What are Performing Rights Organizations (PROs)?

Performing rights societies (PRS) also known as Performing Rights Organizations (PRO), collect and distribute royalties for the public performance of musical works.

## Why Do Artists Need to Register with their PRO?

Artists and record labels need to register their works with a PRO, or Performance Rights Organization, to ensure they are properly compensated for the use of their music. PROs collect and distribute royalties on behalf of songwriters, composers, and publishers when their music is played publicly, whether it be on radio, television, live performances, or streaming services. By registering their works with a PRO, artists and record labels can ensure that they receive the royalties they are owed for the use of their music, and that they are able to track and monitor the use of their music. Additionally, many venues and businesses are required by law to have licenses with PROs to play copyrighted music, so by registering with a PRO, artists and record labels can ensure their music is legally played in these settings.

## How do PROs Collect and Distribute Artists' Royalties?

A Performing Rights Society (PRO) collects royalties for the public performance of music on behalf of its members, which include independent artists and record labels. The PRO does this by monitoring the usage of music in various media, such as television, radio, and live performances, and then collecting royalties from the entities that use the music, such as broadcasters and venues. The PRO then distributes the royalties collected to its members based on the usage of their music. This typically involves tracking the usage of each song and determining how much each member should be paid based on the usage of their music. The PRO will also keep records of the usage of songs to ensure accurate distribution of royalties to the right copyright owners. The PRO also provides an online portal for the independent artists and record labels to check their royalties and usage of their songs.

### Action Step

In most countries, the local Performing Rights Organization operate as non-profits. A lot of PROs are quite approachable and accessible for indie musicians. Check out their website and read through the FAQ section and contact their customer support line with any questions you might have.

# CHAPTER TEN

# SOUND RECORDING VS. SONG WRITING

U nderstanding the difference between royalties and rights for recorded music vs. the royalties and rights of an artist's lyrics and compositions.

## The Basics of a Sound Recording

A sound recording is a recording of a performance of a musical work, usually recorded on a medium such as a CD, tape, or digital file. This includes the recorded performance of musicians, singers, and any other sounds that are captured during the recording process. Sound recordings are protected by copyright, and the owner of the sound recording has the exclusive right to reproduce, distribute, and publicly perform the recording.

## The Basics of Songwriting Rights

On the other hand, songwriting refers to the composition of a musical work, which includes the lyrics and melody of a song. The songwriting is protected by copyright, and the owner of the songwriting has the exclusive right to reproduce, distribute, and publicly perform the song. Additionally, the songwriting copyright owner has the right to authorize others to make sound recordings of the song. This means that the songwriting copyright owner has the right to control how their song is used, and to be paid for its use.

## The Difference Between Songs/Compositions and Sound Recordings

In summary, a sound recording is a recording of a performance of a song, while songwriting refers to the composition of a musical work, including lyrics and melody. The rights of the two are different and protected by copyright. The owner of a sound recording has the exclusive rights to reproduce, distribute, and publicly perform the recording, whereas the owner of the song has the exclusive rights to reproduce, distribute, and publicly perform the song, as well as the ability to authorize others to make sound recordings of the song.

In most cases, record labels deal primarily with sound recordings and leave song publishing to the artist to manage themselves or through a third-party music publisher.

### Action Step

Encourage your artists (this also applies to you if you are an artist/songwriter) to keep track of "who is in the room" when a song is written. There are many disputes that occur over who wrote a specific song, especially if that song starts earning significant publishing income. When co-writing with another writer (or a group of writers), take a photo and a note of who is present and the percentage of their contributions.

## Conclusion

Music publishing is an essential aspect of the music industry that plays a crucial role in protecting and promoting the rights of composers and songwriters. A music publishing company is a business that owns and manages the rights to a collection of musical compositions and licenses the use of those compositions to other parties, such as record labels, film studios, and other music users. They are responsible for protecting the rights of the composers and songwriters and ensuring that they receive royalties for the use of their work. Record labels, on the other hand, are responsible for producing, manufacturing, distributing, and promoting the recorded music. By understanding the role of music publishing and how it works, record labels can better navigate the complex landscape of the music industry and make more informed decisions about the music they release and the artists they sign.

Music publishing can be a great opportunity for record labels to diversify their income streams since they can acquire the rights to songs and license them to other music users. Moreover, by working closely with music publishing companies, record labels can access a wider pool of talented composers and songwriters, which could lead to discovering new hit songs.

In short, music publishing is an integral part of the music industry and understanding it can be beneficial for record labels in terms of revenue diversification and discovering new talent. It is important for record labels to have a good understanding of the music publishing landscape and to build relationships with reputable music publishing companies.

I hope this small book has helped demystify the world of music publishing for you and your record label. However, there is so much more for us to learn in this space. Attend conferences, network with other record labels, and indie musicians. Keep learning, especially when it comes to the complicated parts of the industry like music publishing. Knowledge is power!

## Additional Resources

**Trusted Vendors, Attorneys, Service Providers**
- Visit our Directory to access a short list of hand-picked industry vendors that can help you and your artists with things like bio writing, royalty accounting, mastering, music law, and radio promotions.
Visit: otherrecordlabels.com/directory

**Bandcamp Resources -** I keep a regularly updated resource page on how to utilize Bandcamp as an independent record label or musician that includes more helpful tips as well as an interview with Andrew Jervis of Bandcamp!
Visit: otherrecordlabels.com/bandcamp

**Book Recommendations -** I constantly maintain a list of music industry and business books that I think will help you in your record label journey.
Visit: otherrecordlabels.com/books

**Record Label Toolkit -** Get access to sample recording contracts, marketing checklist, release roadmap, and a free record label business plan.
Visit: otherrecordlabels.com/toolkit

**Record Label Facebook Community -** Join our private Facebook group for independent record label employees and owners.
Visit: facebook.otherrecordlabels.com

**Be Your Own Record Label -** A resource for independent artists who self-manage their own career to discover what they can learn from record labels.
Visit: otherrecordlabels.com/toolbox

**Digital Distribution -** My favorite digital distributor geared towards smaller, independent record labels: 3tone Music.
Learn More: otherrecordlabels.com/distro

# Music Publishing FAQs

## What is a publishing administrator?

A music publishing administrator is a company or individual who helps songwriters and copyright holders manage and collect royalties from the use of their musical works. They typically handle tasks such as registering songs with performing rights organizations, licensing songs for use in films, television shows, and commercials, and collecting and distributing royalties to the copyright holder. They also handle other related tasks such as tracking where and how the songs are used and providing detailed reports on the earnings generated by the songs. They may also help songwriters and copyright holders negotiate better terms and royalty rates with users of their works and help to protect the copyright holder's rights. In summary, a music publishing administrator helps songwriters and copyright holders to manage and collect royalties from the use of their musical works, and provides a variety of services such as licensing, tracking, and reporting, that facilitates the administration of the songs.

## What is SoundExchange?

SoundExchange is a non-profit performance rights organization (PRO) in the United States that collects and distributes royalties for the use of sound recordings. It was created in 2000 as part of the Digital Millennium Copyright Act (DMCA) to provide a way for copyright holders of sound recordings to be compensated for the use of their recordings on certain digital platforms such as satellite radio, internet radio, and cable TV music channels.

SoundExchange is responsible for collecting and distributing royalties from these digital platforms and other non-interactive streaming services, like Pandora, Spotify, and SiriusXM. These royalties are paid to the copyright holders of sound recordings and the featured artists and are separate from the royalties paid to the songwriters and publishers for the use of their compositions. SoundExchange also provides detailed reports to its members, helping them to monitor the use of their recordings and ensure they are being properly compensated.

## Do I need to register my record label with a PRO?

A record label does not typically need to register with a Performing Rights Organization (PRO) to collect performance royalties for the songs on their label's releases. However, it is the responsibility of the copyright holder or the publisher of the songs to register with a PRO so that the songs can be tracked, and royalties can be collected for the public performances of the songs. In most cases, the copyright holder is the songwriter or the publisher, but if the record label also owns the copyright, they can also register with a PRO.

## Do I need to mail a copy of my music to myself for it to be copyrighted?

The practice of mailing a copy of your music to yourself, also known as the "poor man's copyright," is a myth and is not a legally recognized way to establish copyright. In the United States, copyright protection is automatically granted to original works as soon as they are fixed in a tangible form, meaning that as soon as you record your music, it is protected by copyright. Therefore, mailing yourself a copy of your music does not provide any additional legal protection or evidence of copyright.

The correct way to register a copyright in the US is by filling out the appropriate forms and sending them along with a non-returnable copy of the work, plus a fee to the US Copyright Office. This process gives you additional benefits such as the ability to sue for infringement, the ability to recover statutory damages, and attorney's fees.

It's worth noting that, even though mailing yourself a copy of your music will not give you any additional legal protection, it's still a good practice to keep records of your creations and evidence of your authorship in case of disputes.

## What is a PRO?

A performance rights organization (PRO) – sometimes referred to as a performing rights society – collects royalties on behalf of songwriters. They receive performance fees from entities who wish to use copyrighted works publicly like on television, radio, or in retail stores. These performance royalties are then paid to the songwriters and publishers. Most countries have their own PROs. For example, in Canada, the local PRO is called SOCAN. In the UK, the PRO is called PRS.

## What is the difference between an ISWC and an ISRC?

An ISWC stands for International Standard Musical Work Code, and is generally given to a unique composition, and is issued by your PRO when you initially register the song. ISRC stands for International Standard Recording Code and is given to a specific recording. These codes are provided by your mastering engineer or your digital distributor (CD Baby, TuneCore, DistroKid, 3Tone Music).

Here's an example: John Smith writes an original song called, "I Love You" and registers it with his PRO, in this case ASCAP in the United States. ASCAP provides John with an ISWC code for the new composition. John then records his new song in a studio and uploads the master recording to the streaming platforms using his digital distributor CD

Baby. Upon registering this single for distribution, CD Baby automatically assigns the song an ISRC.

It should be noted that these codes are completely unrelated. CD Baby does not require an ISWC to distribute a recording. Similarly, John's performing rights organization (ASCAP) does not need to know his ISRC.

**What is SoundTrust?**

SoundTrust is a global independent music rights management company that helps rights holders to manage and monetize their music rights. They offer a range of services including royalty collection, licensing, and administration, as well as data and analytics to help rights holders understand and optimize their revenue streams.

Whether a record label should register with SoundTrust would depend on the specific needs of the label and the type of rights they hold. If the label has a diverse catalogue of music and is looking to maximize their revenue from royalties and licensing, then registering with SoundTrust could be beneficial. SoundTrust can help the label to manage and monetize their rights, as well as provide them with data and analytics to better understand their revenue streams.

It's worth noting that SoundTrust is not a Performing Rights Organization (PRO), but rather a rights management company that can help with the administration and collection of royalties for the music of their clients (record labels and artists) from different PROs around the world, and from other income streams not related to PROs.

## What is SoundReef?

Soundreef is an Italian-based independent music rights management company. It is a Performing Rights Organization (PRO) that helps rights holders to manage and monetize their music rights. They offer a range of services including royalty collection, licensing, and administration, as well as data and analytics to help rights holders understand and optimize their revenue streams. They also provide a platform for the management of the rights and the distribution of royalties to the creators, the performers, and the publishers.

Soundreef operates in several European countries and in some countries outside of Europe, and it's open to any rights holder, including independent musicians, record labels, publishers, and others. It's an alternative for those rights holders that are not satisfied with their current PRO or for those who want to join a PRO but doesn't want to be tied to a specific geographical area.

Soundreef's goal is to provide a more transparent and efficient service for rights holders, and to help them maximize their revenue from royalties and licensing.

**What are Neighboring Rights?**

Neighboring Rights - Neighboring rights refer to the rights of performers and producers of sound recordings to receive royalties for the use of their performances and productions. These rights are separate from the rights of songwriters and publishers, who receive royalties for the use of their compositions. Performers and producers of sound recordings have the right to be compensated for the use of their performances and productions, whether it's on radio, television, streaming services, or other public performances. These rights are often referred to as "neighboring rights" because they are closely related to the rights of copyright holders, but they are distinct from them. Neighboring rights royalties are collected by performance rights organizations and then distributed to the performers and producers. In the United States, neighboring rights do apply to some degree. The United States has recognized some of the rights that are associated with neighboring rights, such as the rights of performers and sound recording copyright owners to be compensated for the use of their performances and productions. However, the scope of neighboring rights in the US is more limited compared to other countries where neighboring rights are considered a distinct set of rights separate from copyright. In the US, these rights are typically covered by statutory licenses, and the royalties are collected and distributed by organizations such as SoundExchange. Additionally, there are some aspects of neighboring rights that are not fully recognized or protected in the US, such as the rights of producers.

## Who do you use to manage your publishing catalog?

I use my friends at 3Tone Publishing (UK) to collect publishing royalties on my behalf (as a songwriter and artist). Visit: 3tonepublishing.co.uk

**Other Record Labels Podcast**
*The Art and Culture of Running a Record Label*

Listen to interviews and insights from today's independent record labels including Sub Pop Records, Asthmatic Kitty Records, Mute Records, Ghostly International, Z Tapes, Asian Man Records, Jagjaguar, and more!

*Listen wherever you get your podcasts.*

**otherrecordlabels.com/listen**

# About the Author

**Scott Orr** is the host of *Other Record Labels*, a podcast about the art and culture of running a record label. Scott also runs Other Songs, a label he started in 2010. He lives and works in Ontario, Canada.

Instagram: @otherrecordlabels, @scott.orr

# Music Publishing Glossary

**Copyright:** The legal right that grants the creators of original works the exclusive right to reproduce, distribute, and display their work. Copyright is the foundation of music publishing, as it gives the publisher the right to license the use of the compositions.

**Mechanical rights:** The right to reproduce a song in a physical format, such as on a CD or vinyl record, or in a digital format, such as on a streaming platform.

**Performance rights:** The right to perform a song publicly, such as in a live concert, on television, or on the radio.

**Synchronization rights:** The right to use a song in conjunction with visual media, such as in a film, television show, or commercial.

**Royalty:** A payment made to the copyright owner of a song for the use of that song.

**Catalog:** A collection of songs owned by a music publishing company.

**Administration:** The process of tracking the use of songs, collecting royalties, and ensuring that the compositions are properly registered with performance rights organizations.

**Co-publishing agreement:** An agreement between a songwriter and a music publishing company where the company provides administrative and creative support in exchange for a percentage of the song's copyright ownership.

**One-Stop:** A music publishing company that owns or controls the rights to multiple songs and can license all the rights for a particular song.

**Public Domain:** The status of a song that is no longer protected by copyright and can be used without permission or payment of royalties.

# MORE BOOKS BY **OTHER RECORD LABELS**

**otherrecordlabels.com/book**

## **Online Courses** for Record Labels

otherrecordlabels.com/courses

# Notes

# Notes

# Notes

# Notes

otherrecordlabels.com

Printed in Great Britain
by Amazon